I'm going to be a...

VET

AUTUMN
PUBLISHING

Written by Marnie Willow
Illustrated by Junissa Bianda
Additional artwork by Hazel Quintanilla

Designed by Lee Italiano
Edited by Helen Catt

Copyright © 2020 Igloo Books Ltd

Published in 2021
First published in the UK by Autumn Publishing
An imprint of Igloo Books Ltd
Cottage Farm, NN6 0BJ, UK
Owned by Bonnier Books
Sveavägen 56, Stockholm, Sweden

Manufactured in China. 0721 001
10 9 8 7 6 5 4 3 2 1

Library of Congress Cataloging-in-Publication
Data is available upon request.

ISBN 978-1-80022-864-1
autumnpublishing.co.uk
bonnierbooks.co.uk

I'm going to be a...
VET

AUTUMN
PUBLISHING

When I grow up, I'm going to be a
vet!

I'll look after animals who are hurt or sick,
so they can **feel** all better.

People will
bring their
sick pets
to my special
surgery.

Young and old,
big and small,
I'm going to
treat them
all!

First, I'll find out why a furry feline's feeling funny.

Then I'll take a temperature and do some tests. I'll work out which tablets and pills will help an ill pup.

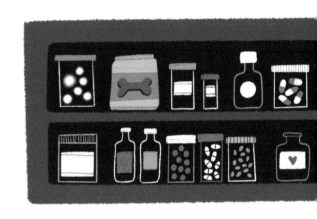

I'll be there when baby animals have their first trips to the vet.

I'll give them their shots and check their weight. They'll get lots of special hugs...

... and maybe a treat or two.

Big animals also need lots of looking after.

I'll help cows with colds...

... and horses with headaches.

There'll be no fevers in the farmyard or sniffles in the stables when I'm the vet in charge.

Maybe I'll work at the zoo, too!

Everyone will be amazed when I help a mother panda give birth to tiny twins.

I'll give them quiet hugs and keep them clean and safe...

... while Mommy Panda has
a very well-earned rest!

Or I'll go wild and travel the world!
If there's an aardvark with an earache, or an elephant
with a wonky trunk...

... or a dozy, snoozy zebra, or a gnu who's hurt his knee, I'll be the one to patch them up and send them running free.

If underwater animals need a helping hand, I'll be ready to dive right in.

(Although, when I'm swimming, it'll be a little tricky to keep the cough syrup in the spoon.)

I'll study really, really hard!
I'll read great **big** books with even
bigger words...

... like

hippopotamus borborygmus

(which is the clever way of saying a hippo's got a rumbly tummy)

I'll learn lots about science and how to make medicine.

Perhaps I'll come up with a brand-new tablet...

... to banish a **tiger's** toothache.

ZOO PUZZLE

When I grow up,
I'll do all these things.

But I've got lots
of other things
to do first.

BEING A
VET

Vets look after animals, just like doctors look after people. They check animals over, and if they're sick or hurt, they do tests to find out why. Then they give them medicine to help them feel better. Some vets look after people's pets. Others work with farm animals. Some work at zoos and aquariums. Others travel the world to look after and learn about animals in the wild.

Vets study very hard for a long time to learn the best ways to treat different animals. Some vets spend all their time studying new and better ways to keep animals healthy. There's lots of ways to be a vet. What will you decide to do?